EXECUTIVE EDITOR
Suzanne Tise-Isoré

EDITORIAL ASSISTANT
Joy Sulitzer

EDITORIAL COORDINATION
Nathalie Chapuis

GRAPHIC DESIGN
Bernard Lagacé

TRANSLATED FROM FRENCH BY
Deke Dusinberre

PROOFREADING
Marc Feustel

PRODUCTION
Élodie Conjat-Cuvelier

COLOR SEPARATION
Bussière, Paris

PRINTED BY
Graphart, Trieste

TT
505
.A1
N53
2010

Distributed in North America by Rizzoli International Publications, Inc.

Simultaneously published in French as *Cristóbal Balenciaga, Philippe Venet,*
Hubert de Givenchy au château des princes de Beauvau Craon.
© Flammarion SA, Paris, 2010

English-language edition
© Flammarion SA, Paris, 2010

Flammarion SA
87, quai Panhard et Levassor
75647 Paris Cedex 13
France
www.editions.flammarion.com

Dépôt légal: 05/2010
10 11 12 3 2 1
ISBN: 9782080301673
Printed in Italy by Graphart

Cristóbal
Balenciaga
Philippe Venet
Hubert de
Givenchy

GRAND
TRADITIONS
OF
FRENCH
COUTURE

Christiane de Nicolay-Mazery

PHOTOGRAPHS BY Luc Castel

Château of the Princes of Beauvau Craon

Flammarion

Contents

A dream has now come true thanks to my friends Hubert de Givenchy and Philippe Venet, who have earned my sincere gratitude. It is an honor for the château of Haroué to host, for the first time in the history of fashion, these three great designers all at once.

I would also like to thank my friend Christiane. Her talent and enthusiasm have turned what was to have been a straightforward exhibition catalogue into a "gem of a book" that I'm sure readers will cherish.

MINNIE, PRINCESS OF BEAUVAU CRAON

What a delight to be able to display these evening gowns in a setting as glamorous as the château of Haroué. It is not just an ancestral home but a jewel of French architectural heritage—a place of history, grandeur, and beauty.

HUBERT DE GIVENCHY

In order to celebrate the recent enhancement of the wonderful family château in Haroué, Hubert de Givenchy suggested to Minnie, princess of Beauvau Craon, that she host an exhibition of evening gowns in a tribute to three designers who left their mark on the history of fashion. The result is a sparkling dialogue between haute couture and a gem of French architectural heritage.

His suggestion was typical of Givenchy's penchant for new challenges, for "making things happen," for a constant quest for beauty that requires tireless creativity. It also reflects his keen sense of friendship. Princess Minnie, meanwhile, was delighted to contribute her own elegance and radiance to her illustrious family's noble residence.

Built between 1720 and 1732 by architect Germain Boffrand for Prince Marc of Beauvau Craon, the château of Haroué was subsequently embellished by major artists of the "golden age" of Lorraine (today a region of France). Haroué benefited from a dazzling court life.

I planned this diminutive book as a reminder of those precious "compacts," those little cases of gold, enamel, or mother-of-pearl that people gave one another in centuries past as a sign of friendship. Its pages create links between the majestic architecture, the glamorous furnishings, the family portraits, the velvet and silken wall linings, and the world of haute couture. Brocades, organzas, shantungs, charmeuse satins, and embroideries mirror paintings, sculptures, bronzes, and rare artifacts. Gowns and objets d'art whisper secrets to each other across the centuries, speaking of elegance and beauty.

An exclusive feature of this exhibition is the famous black satin dress—one of three copies—worn by Audrey Hepburn in the film *Breakfast at Tiffany's*. Hubert de Givenchy had the privilege of meeting Hepburn as a very young man, and he worked with her throughout her life. You only have to look at Audrey's smile to hear her saying to Hubert, "You're my best friend, so I'll watch over you now that I'm among the stars."

CHRISTIANE DE NICOLAY-MAZERY

Cristóbal Balenciaga

The handsome Cristóbal Balenciaga was born in the
Spanish Basque country in 1895. His father was a
fisherman, his mother was a seamstress who worked at
home for wealthy families on vacation. As a small boy
Cristóbal liked to watch his mother work with fabrics, and
he became fascinated with tailoring. It was said that at age
five, for want of a real customer, he used his dog as a model
and made a four-legged coat. A few years later, aged seven
or so, he saw the highly elegant countess of Casa Torrès—
grandmother of Belgium's Queen Fabiola—in his
hometown where she spent the summer; the lad allegedly
said to the countess, "Me, too, I can make something
beautiful like that." Taking him at his word, she ordered a
dress, becoming his first client. Ten years later, his parents
finally allowed him to go to San Sebastián to study fashion
design. That was where he opened his first business, in 1919,
at the age of 24 years, before moving on to Madrid and
then to Paris, in 1937, where he set up his fashion house
on Avenue George V.

PAGES 10–11 Main façade of the château of Harouë.
FACING PAGE Cristóbal Balenciaga, 1927.

"Everything and anything has been said about Balenciaga—he hid his mystery beneath great simplicity." HUBERT DE GIVENCHY

ABOVE: Cristóbal Balenciaga, circa 1952.

Success came early. People admired Balenciaga's elegance, his sense of tailoring, his perfect technique, and his innovative ideas. He could have been a sculptor—he sculpted his garments on the bodies of his models. He insisted on complete silence during his creative sessions, while his eyes and hands roved over the living forms that so inspired him. Balenciaga disliked both publicity and journalists, and he refused to be photographed. "Why take my photograph?" he would ask, "I'm not some famous scientist or victorious general." Reserved, secretive, quiet, he liked to be alone, to think and reflect. "Flee the world," he advised, if you want to be creative. And in fact Balenciaga led an almost monastic life, totally devoted to his explorations into fashion. During his fashion shows, no music would be played; his tall, elegant, majestic models would stride quickly, not looking at the audience. Balenciaga would remain behind the white curtain, noting the audience reaction, then would leave. Yet he displayed a Spanish spirit that surfaced in the dark reds and deep blacks of his native country, a fiery spirit wed to the subtle refinement of French artistry, combining the architecture of shapes with the finesse of fabrics and colors.

All the most elegant women wanted to be dressed by Balenciaga—queens, oriental princesses, the duchess of Windsor, and other chic American women such as Mrs. Paul Mellon. Then there was Countess Mona Bismarck, who in 1963 ordered eighty-eight of his designs—followed the next year by no fewer than one hundred and forty orders.

Behind his great reserve, Balenciaga was a man of great generosity, goodness, and sensitivity. He was both totally classic and totally modern—indeed, he was the first to propose haute-couture shorts. And he remains one of the greatest designers of our age.

When Doña Fabiola de Mora y Aragón married King Baudouin I of Belgium on December 15, 1960, she became the fifth queen of the Belgians. Born in Madrid to a noble Spanish family, she had known Balenciaga since her childhood. Her grandmother, the countess of Casa Torrès, had encouraged the lad when he was just the son of a fisherman. Later, the young ladies of the Mora y Aragón family all attended their debutant balls in gowns designed by Balenciaga. For her own wedding—a love match—the new Queen Fabiola wore a majestic silk satin bridal gown made by her favorite designer. The royal wedding took place in the Cathedral of Saints Michael and Gudula in Brussels and, a first for the times, it was broadcast on television.

"*Watching a Balenciaga fitting was like watching a miracle: when you saw his dresses, they didn't seem to have been touched. They floated, they moved, they created mystery.*" HUBERT DE GIVENCHY

PAGES 24–25 Child musicians sculpted by Barthélemy Guibal lead to the main courtyard of the château of the princes of Beauvau Craon, whose façade was built in 1720 by Gabriel Boffrand. The other façade overlooks the formal garden and groves.
PAGE 27 Long dress of black charmeuse satin with a cloak of emerald ostrich feathers, 1961.
PAGES 28–29 Opposite the foliage, a pink tulle dress re-embroidered with flowers of silken thread.
PAGES 30–31 AND 35 Rabbit and squirrel in the dining room in Haroué—details from paintings of the four seasons done by Baron François Gérard for Louis XVIII.
FACING PAGE A bouquet of flowers in *pietre dure* adorns the mantelpiece of the Pillement tower.

*"M*onsieur Balenciaga's work is conjugated in the present—we always go on discovering his wonderful path toward stunning beauty."* EMMANUEL UNGARO

The princess of Beauvau Craon, née Minnie Gregorini Bingham, is the grandmother of the current owner. In 1920, the princess decided to bring the château of Haroué back to life following many years of disuse. "If it's possible to be reborn within your own lifetime, then I'd say when I was twenty and left Italy to embrace France wholeheartedly, I took root in Lorraine and began life again there, where my life assumed its real purpose."

PAGES 34–37 A detail of chinoiserie and rococo decoration in the Pillement tower; a jacket of raspberry tulle embroidered with crystals and gold thread, 1963.
PAGES 40–43 A dress of faille and lace re-embroidered with jet; a Tiffany coffee service, a Murano glass dish, and several porcelain cups painted by Inès de Nicolay sit on a silver tray.

"When a woman takes a step,
it is her dress that walks, and when she dances it
is her dress that dances." CRISTÓBAL BALENCIAGA

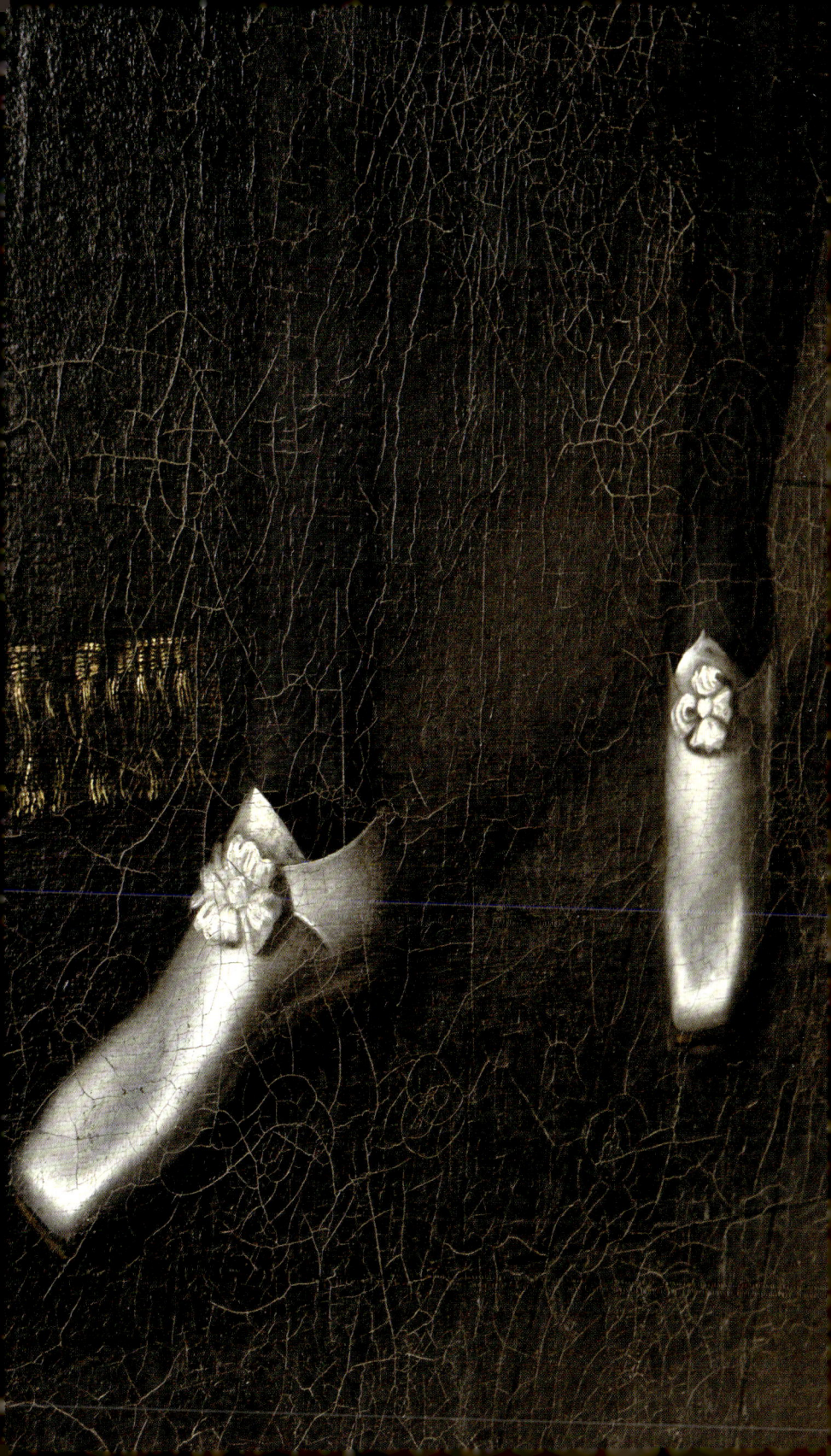

PAGES 48–49 Detail of a vase of Chinese porcelain and gilded
bronze; evening gown of shantung and fuchsia lace, 1961.
ABOVE Sketch for the summer 1961 collection by Lucia,
Balenciaga's *première d'atelier* (head of studio).
FACING PAGE Winter 1958 collection, photographed by Tom Kublin.
PAGES 52–53 In 1858, the artist Antoine Hébert decorated the Salon
Doré (Gold Drawing Room) to welcome Emperor Napoleon III.
He was assisted by Ludmilla, princess of Beauvau, and her three
sisters including Delphine, the countess of Potocka, who had
studied under Chopin. The ladies devised this decorative
scheme of the muses, seasons, and months, which included
their own portraits.

Philippe Venet

Born in Lyon, France, as a young man Philippe Venet went to work for Pierre Court, the only tailor authorized to execute designs by Cristóbal Balenciaga. Venet remained in Lyon for several years, acquiring a perfect cutting technique that favored a simple and spare yet terribly elegant structure. In 1951, he became an assistant designer for Schiaparelli, one of the most influential designers of the 1930s whose profoundly innovative ideas, tinged with surrealism, had a considerable impact on haute couture. There Venet met Hubert de Givenchy; when Givenchy opened his own fashion house in 1952, he invited Venet to join him.

In 1962, aged thirty-three, Venet started his own house. His tailoring was not only perfect but imaginative. The 1960s were marked by his "kite" coats whereas his designs of the 1980s and 1990s were appealing for their fresh, lively colors. His evening gowns were romantic and sophisticated, his designs consistently youthful, colorful, and joyful. American women loved his startling coats as

FACING PAGE Philippe Venet, 1970.

well as his long, flowering dresses of light materials and bright colors. Twice a year he showed his collection in the United States, in Los Angeles and New York.

Venet has a taste for essentials—his perfect construction and technique is combined with an inventiveness that appeals to young women. Meanwhile, his personal charm, kindness, and sensitivity make him an artist of faultless tact. In 1985 he won French haute couture's Dé d'Or (Gold Thimble) award. As a mark of his long personal friendship with the princess of Beauvau Craon, for whom he designed a magnificent bridal gown with long train and veil of old lace in 1978, he presented her in 2008 with large velvet table covers bearing the Beauvau Craon coat of arms, which today adorn the arms room at Haroué.

ABOVE Philippe Venet, 1990.

*"*H*is great discretion,
sweetness, dignity, talent, and loyalty make
Philippe an incredible friend."*

MINNIE DE BEAUVAU CRAON

ABOVE Minnie on her wedding day, July 1, 1978, photographed in the raw
shantung dress designed by her friend, Philippe Venet.
FACING PAGE The main staircase at Haroué photographed by Ali Von Bothmer.

PAVILLON DE ROHAN

Auguste DONNY fils

Tailleur

37, Rue du Faubourg Saint-Honoré, 37

PARIS

PHILIPPE VENET

HISTOIRE GÉNÉALOGIQUE

MAISON DE BEAUVAU

DEDIÉÉ

à aut et Tres Puissant Seigneur
Marquis de Beauvau de Craon
uier de Lorraine

s Maisons qui soyent exemptes de la Critique Sur leur
à beaucoup qui appuyent leur origine Sur des faits Si extra
ent plûtost a la fable qu'a la verité, la Maison de Beauvau
, et de la Critique et de la fable. Vous n'avez Monsieur
le voir le traité que j'en ay fait au commencement de cette

On December 16, 1704, Anne-Marguerite
de Ligniville married Marc de Beauvau, prince of Craon.
Anne-Marguerite was a countess of the Holy Roman
Empire, and at eighteen was a lady-in-waiting to the
duchess of Lorraine. Beautiful, sweet, and pleasant, she also
loved the arts. She therefore summoned Jean Lamour
to do the wonderful wrought-iron work for the château's
entrance gate, the banister of the main staircase, and
window sills with their entwined double-C motif.

PAGES 60–61 Dress of white crepe, 1989; Minnie Gregorini, princess of Beauvau,
grandmother of the current owner, photographed by Horst P. Horst in the 1930s.
PAGE 62 The linen room contains not only old hat boxes but also Princess Minnie's
wedding dress, designed by Philippe Venet.
PAGE 64 Dress of black and white crepe, 1988.
PAGE 65 The mahogany box containing the livery buttons with the coats of arms
of the Beauvau and Gregorini families.
PAGES 66–67 Seventeenth-century engraved crystal glass opposite the Beauvau Ligniville
coat of arms in the large genealogical volume on the princes of Beauvau Craon.
PAGES 68–69 Built on the foundations of a twelfth-century castle, today's Beauvau
residence is surrounded by deep moats; dress of emerald-green lamé, 1991.

"*Isn't a fashion designer like a magician who creates illusions—and perhaps beauty?*" HUBERT DE GIVENCHY

Hubert de Givenchy

Born in the city of Beauvais in northern France in 1927, Hubert de Givenchy was only two when his father died. From childhood he was sensitive to beauty of all kinds. His mother was a musician and his grandfather, Jules Badin, ran the Gobelins and Beauvais tapestry workshops. Like Balenciaga, at an early age Givenchy knew that he wanted to become a fashion designer and enter the world of haute couture, but his mother asked him to complete his education first.

Once he graduated from secondary school, the young Givenchy applied for a job with Jacques Fath. At the same time, he enrolled in the school of fine arts. Fath would go around in a long gray wolf-fur overcoat, wearing Iris Noir scent. At Fath's, Givenchy discovered an enchanting world full of fantasy, gaiety, and inventiveness. Later, he would work for Piguet and Lelong, before moving to Schiaparelli in 1947, where he spent four years of total creative freedom and happiness. There he met the highly elegant and sophisticated ladies who would remain his faithful clients,

FACING PAGE Hubert de Givenchy and Audrey Hepburn during a fitting for Fred Zinneman's film, *The Nun's Story*, 1959.

such as Daisy Fellowes, Babe Paley, the duchess
of Windsor, Lady Abdy, Countess Gazzoni Frascara,
Barbara Hutton, Patricia Lopez, and Gloria Guinness.

On January 4, 1952, aged just twenty-four, Hubert
de Givenchy opened his own fashion house at 8 rue Alfred
de Vigny in Paris. It met with swift success. People liked
the youthful elegance and harmonious atmosphere that
reigned there. Givenchy's models were ravishing—the
marvelous Bettina Grazziani lent appeal to everything, for
she was beautiful, fresh, and young, and wore his designs
wonderfully.

In 1953, a long-anticipated meeting finally took place in
New York, between Givenchy and Balenciaga. Givenchy
had boundless admiration for the man he considered his
"mentor." A great friendship was born, one that would

ABOVE Hubert de Givenchy, 1998.

last until Balenciaga's death in 1972. They became a close pair who compared sketches and mutually advised and criticized one another. "Balenciaga was the great technical revelation of my career, because he never took the easy route.… Before meeting him, I would play with fabrics—but then, my eyes were opened."

Another decisive encounter for Givenchy was Audrey Hepburn, his ray of sunshine. The doe-eyed actress would become his muse, his fairy godmother, his friend forever. She was all charm, grace, and kindness. In all her movie contracts after *Sabrina*, she insisted on being dressed by her friend, Hubert de Givenchy. The designer also dressed Lauren Bacall, Elizabeth Taylor, Jean Seberg, Marlene Dietrich, Capucine, the duchess of Devonshire, Mrs. Whitney, Mrs. Paul Mellon, Jacqueline Kennedy, Princess Grace of Monaco, Maria Callas, and others. His clients often became his great friends.

Twice a year, Givenchy examined hundreds of samples. After having smelled, touched, draped, and shaped the fabric on the body of his models, he was ready to conceive his next collection. The Givenchy style was an alliance between pure, classic lines and high quality fabrics, whether lavish or light, black or colored (not forgetting instants of purest white). "The more elaborate the fabric," he would say, "the simpler the shape."

His ravishing models wore his youthful, flowing designs—influenced by floral and foliate ideas—with perfect grace. Dresses of strict elegance appeared side by side with fanciful outfits embroidered with polka dots, lily-of-the-valley, clover, lemons, or wild strawberries—Givenchy has always been a nature-lover. Even today he continues to be passionate about his art collection, his country home, his garden—anything that brings beauty to life.

"*The only things worthy
of interest are the ones that are heartfelt.*"

AUDREY HEPBURN

For *Breakfast at Tiffany's*, Hepburn paid a visit to Hubert de Givenchy and chose from his collection a black dress whose low-cut back she loved. Clothed in this sheath dress, she became the iconic image of the movie itself. Indeed, starting with Billy Wilder's *Sabrina*, Hepburn's contracts insisted that Hubert de Givenchy dress her for all her roles.

Givenchy made three copies of this black dress designed in 1961. Today one is held by the Costume Museum in Madrid, the second was auctioned at Christie's for $920,000 for the benefit of Dominique Lapierre's "City of Joy" charity in Calcutta, and the one on show here is part of the Givenchy fashion house archives.

FACING PAGE AND PAGES 96–99 Shots from *Breakfast at Tiffany's* by Blake Edwards, 1961; Hubert de Givenchy's sketch of the dress worn by Audrey Hepburn in *Breakfast at Tiffany's*.

"*For me, Audrey was a doe-eyed angel. She brought her own grace to the garments she wore.*" HUBERT DE GIVENCHY

"'*To be a gentleman means,
as the word says, you must first be a gentle man,'
she taught us. And that, Givenchy was. Together
they created her look, the externalization of her
style.... As a result of their collaboration,
she has often been referred to as the most elegant,
the most stylish woman in the world. But that
elegance had its roots in both their inner values.
It came from the right place.*" SEAN HEPBURN FERRER

"*Fabrics are living things,
fabrics are my guide—once I drape them,
I begin to dream.*" HUBERT DE GIVENCHY

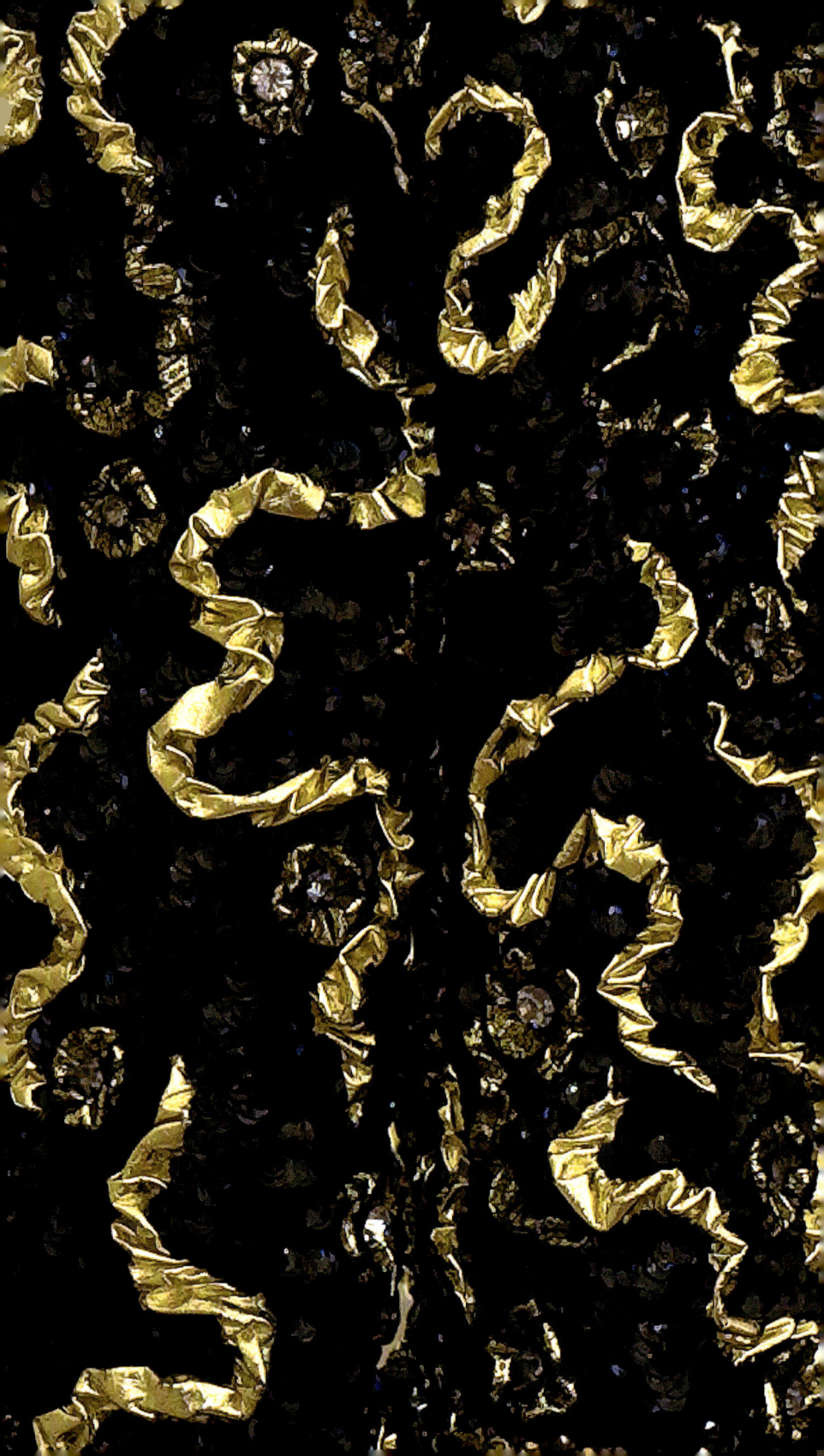

" *The house was soon nicknamed 'the cathedral' because there reigned an atmosphere of seriousness, concentration, and quiet.*"

HUBERT DE GIVENCHY

"*A good fashion designer must be an architect when it comes to plans, a sculptor when it comes to shapes, a painter when it comes to color, a musician when it comes to harmony, and a philosopher when it comes to moderation.*" CRISTÓBAL BALENCIAGA

PAGES 128–129 Photograph of Charles-Louis, prince of Beauvau Craon, taken in 1920; left, his dressing room in Haroué.
PAGE 130 In the main entrance is a full-length portrait of Louis de Beauvau, King Henry IV's lieutenant-general in Burgundy.
FACING PAGE Long dress of black silk jersey with criss-cross effect of gold leather down the sleeves and sides. It was worn by Jerry Hall in 1975.
PAGES 134–135 Detail of pagoda with mandarin in the Pillement tower, opposite a red satin evening gown with open back embroidered with gold thread and jewelry stones.
PAGES 136–137 The handsome colonnade in the main courtyard was designed by Gabriel Boffrand for the prince of Beauvau in 1720.

List of Dresses

DRESSES BY CRISTÓBAL BALENCIAGA

1. Long dress of black charmeuse satin with a cloak of emerald ostrich feathers, 1951.

2. Skirt of black silk faille, white jacket embroidered with large pearls and diamonds, 1952.

3. Dress of coffee-colored faille and little cap re-embroidered with jet and pendants, 1955.

4. Queen Fabiola's wedding dress of ivory duchess satin edged with white mink, 1960. Tiara with brilliant-cut diamonds and long veil of tulle.

5. Little bridesmaid's dress of silver moire with frock-coat of porcelain-blue velvet trimmed with ermine, 1960.

6. Little usher's outfit of blue velvet pants, waistcoat, and shirt of champagne-colored silk, 1960.

7. Evening gown of fuchsia shantung, bodice veiled with lace of matching color, 1961.

8. Pantsuit with white charmeuse satin top and matching belt. Long tulle coat with "sweet pea" re-embroidery, 1962.

9. Long skirt of white satin, jacket of red tulle embroidered with ruby-colored stones, 1963.

10. Long dress of bright pink shot faille, bodice embroidered with strips of red celluloid. Matching jacket, 1964.

11. Evening cloak of tulle and white organza, re-embroidered with white and yellow organdy flowers. Long tunic dress of white chiffon, 1965.

12. Faille dress and jacket with chestnut-colored lace re-embroidered with jet, 1967.

13. Bright yellow faille dress with large flowers embroidered in fuchsia, purple, and yellow velvet chenille flowers, 1967.

14. Pink tulle evening gown entirely re-embroidered with flowers of silken thread, 1967.

DRESSES BY PHILIPPE VENET

15. Dress of black and white crepe, 1988.

16. Dress of amethyst satin, 1988.

17. Long dress of red crepe, 1988.

18. Dress of white crepe, 1989.

19. Dress of pink crepe, 1989.

20. Dress of silver lamé, 1989.

21. Short dress of silver lamé, 1989.

22. Flounce dress of fuchsia satin organza, 1990.

23. Dress of blue, pink, and fuchsia printed organza, 1990.

24. Short dress of purple shantung organza, 1990.

25. Short dress of fuchsia satin organza, 1990.

26. Bridal gown of gold, white, and silver lamé, 1990. Tiara by M. Marant.

27. Dress of black crepe, 1991.

28. Long dress of copper lamé, 1991.

29. Dress of emerald-green lamé, 1991.

DRESSES BY HUBERT DE GIVENCHY

30. The black satin dress worn by Audrey Hepburn in *Breakfast at Tiffany's*, 1961.

31. Black velvet dress and tulle bolero re-embroidered with black vinyl, large diamond, and gold leather, 1970.

32. Jacket of black duchess satin, back embroidered with silk and jet, pants of black gabardine wool, 1972.

33. Evening gown of black velvet and faille skirt, flounce sleeves, 1979.

34. Long dress of black silk jersey, gold criss-cross braiding down sides and sleeves, 1982.

35. Evening cloak-dress of ruby-red satin, open back embroidered with gold thread and stones, 1985.

36. Long cocktail dress of red velvet chenille knit, 1986.

37. Sheath dress of chestnut-brown satin and re-embroidered silver bolero of metallicized leather, 1988.

38. Apricot-colored Moroccan crepe sheath dress embroidered down each side with criss-cross pattern of gold thread, 1990.

39. Ensemble in gold and brown brocade with pockets decorated in filigree work, matching pants, 1991.

40. Dress of black charmeuse silk and jacket of ruffled black velvet edged with diamond braiding, 1993.

41. Ruby-colored satin sheath dress adorned with red rooster feathers, wide belt embroidered with ruby-red vinyl and jewelry stones, undated.

42. Long dress of black velvet guipure, undated.

43. Dress of shantung organza and a bolero with imitation-straw embroidery, undated.

Photographic Credits

Every year the château of Haroué participates in an outdoor opera festival called *Opéra en plein air*, produced by the Akouna company. The performances take place on the first Friday and Saturday in September.

Château of Haroué
54740 Haroué
Tel: (33-3) 83 52 40 14
Fax: (33-3) 83 52 44 19
contact@chateaudeharoue.com
www.chateaudeharoue.com

Acknowledgments

Minnie, princess of Beauvau Craon
would like to thank
Her Majesty Queen Fabiola
of Belgium for allowing
her wedding dress,
designed by Balenciaga,
to be included in the exhibition.

Especially for their crucial support
George Emmanuel
and Queen Ortiz,
Nicola and Lijana Ortiz,
Oliver and Egle Ortiz, and
Serjei and Graziella Sozonoff.

Her deep gratitude to
Madame Sonsoles Diez de Rivera
e Icaza of the Foundation
Cristóbal Balenciaga, Rafael Garcia
Serrano of the Museo del Traje
in Madrid, Maison Givenchy,
Annelise Heinzelman, Véronique
Benitah and Stéphane Marant

Victoria and Sebastian

And to
HSH Princess Armand of Arenberg
Isabelle Baer
Thomas Brzustowfki
Pierre-Yves Caillault
Catherine Charoy
Tristan and Charlotte Duval
Professor François Gicquel
Philippine de Lencquesaing

HH Princess Wanda de Ligne
Sophie Lauriot-Prevost
Édith Marais
Françoise Martin-Haruspuru
Nadine Morano, French
Government Minister
France de Nicolay-Anthonioz
Cléophée and Guillaume Pellerin
Caroline Pigozzi
Linda and Alberto Pinto
Marianne Robic
Bruno Roy
Fabienne de Sèze-Lafon
Claire Stoullig

PATRONS
Dominique Roitel
and Jean-Louis Janin-Daviet
from the Henryot company,
François Renauld from
Assurances Gacon et Associés,
Marie-Christine Neige from
the Printemps department store
in Nancy, and Bérangère de Beco,
president of the Friends
of the château of Haroué.

Dominique Boileau
Jean-Marc Gladysz
Jean-Pierre and Aline Hisler
Marie-Thérèse Magnien
Didier Misler
Jean-Pierre Servillat
Francis Vauthier